"From Stettin in the Baltic to Trieste in the Adriatic,
an iron curtain has descended across the Continent.
Behind that line lie all the capitals of the ancient
states of Central and Eastern Europe. Warsaw, Berlin,
Prague, Vienna, Budapest, Belgrade, Bucharest and
Sofia, all these famous cities and the populations
around them lie in what I must call the Soviet sphere,
and all are subject in one form or another, not only to
Soviet influence but to a very high and, in some cases,
increasing measure of control from Moscow."

Winston Churchill, Westminster College, Fulton,
Missouri, March 5, 1946

DUBLIN

LONDON

PARIS

BARCELONA

COPENHAGEN

HAMBURG

TERDAM

ELS

WEST BERLIN ● EAST BERLIN

BONN

PRAGUE

MUNICH

VIENNA

BERN

BUDAPEST

TRIËSTE

BELGRADE

BUCHAREST

SOFIA

ROME

TIRANA

THE LOST BORDER
BRIAN ROSE
THE LANDSCAPE OF
THE IRON CURTAIN

WITH A FOREWORD BY ANTHONY BAILEY
PRINCETON ARCHITECTURAL PRESS, NEW YORK

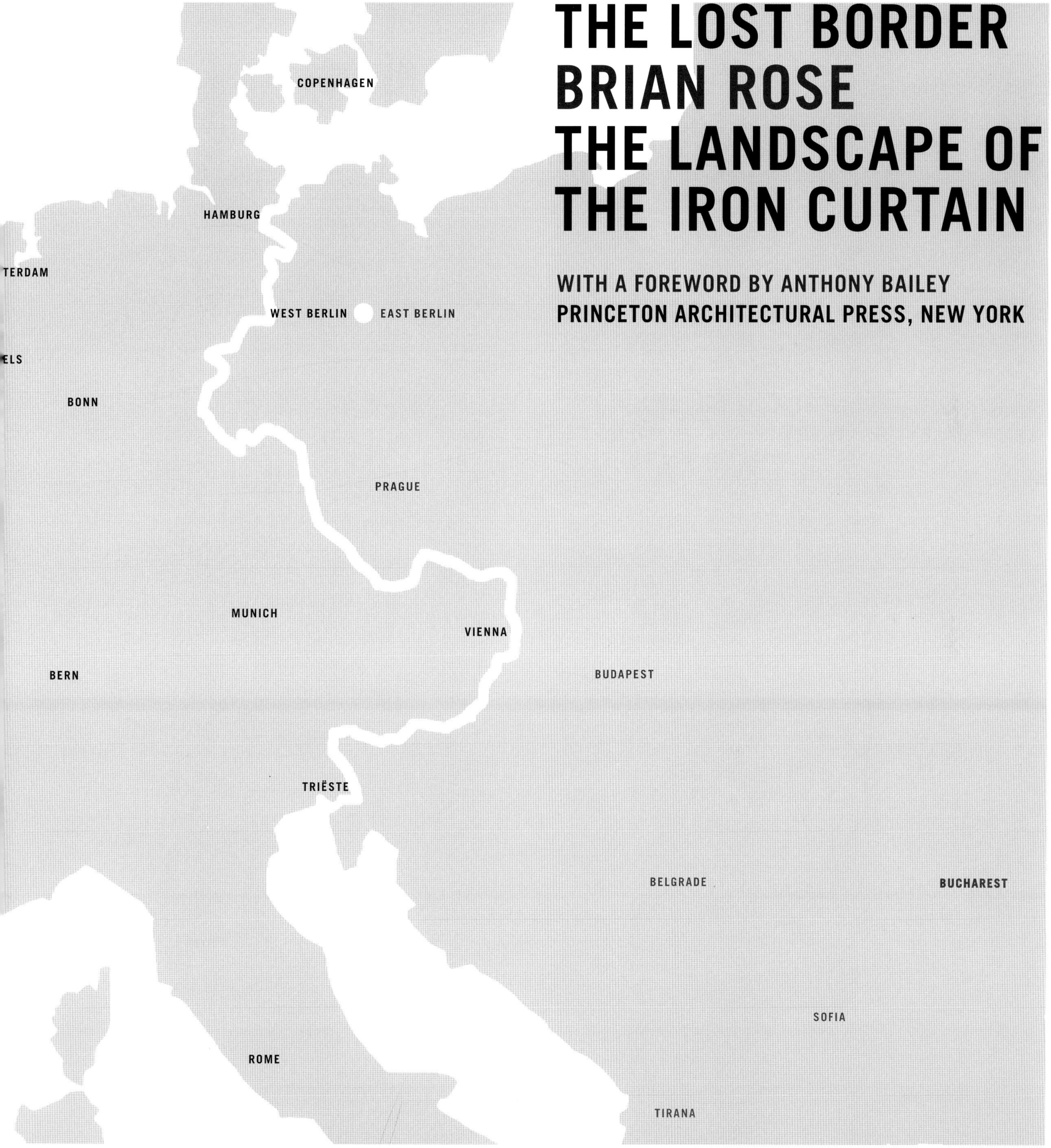

To my son Brendan and my wife Renée Schoonbeek

* * *

I want to express special thanks to Anamarie
Michnevich, who has been friend, creative counsel,
and second set of eyes throughout this project.

FOREWORD
ANTHONY BAILEY

How quickly it disappeared! The Iron Curtain—*die Grenze*, "the border," as West Germans straightforwardly called the German section of the barrier that snaked from north to south across Europe; or the *anti-faschistische Schutzwall*, the wall providing protection against fascism, as the East German regime tendentiously dubbed their menacing wire-and-concrete creation. For at least half a lifetime we thought it was going to be there forever. Then suddenly, in 1989, it was gone. It seems a few moments ago but we are now about to celebrate the fifteenth anniversary of the collapse of the Wall. Memories will be prompted, mementoes brought forth, words and pictures evoked. Brian Rose's photographs should have a starring role in this recollection of our past.

In 1981, during the course of a journey along and sometimes through the Iron Curtain, I talked with many young and middle-aged people in Central and Eastern Europe who believed that the system that enclosed them—including the lethal fence on the west and the wall that ran between the Berlins and surrounded West Berlin—could never change. Yet not everyone, at least on this side, had lost hope. Traveling along the West German border, I came on numerous little lanes that had once joined village to village, farm to farm, and had been turned into cul-de-sacs that ended with border markers, fences, mined strips, watchtowers, and armed guards. In several places I encountered old men who strolled daily down these lanes as far as they could, to gaze at the obscene border. It was always there. But, as one veteran who had experienced the days of Hitler and World War II told me, he had had a superstitious feeling that one day he would walk to the end of the lane and find that, by some magic, *die Grenze* was gone.

In the light of history, this static parenthesis was short. The dividing line first took shape in wartime conferences between the western powers and their then-ally, the Soviet Union, as a possible way of separating occupation zones and spheres of influence in the Third Reich once it had been defeated. The border was slowly hardened in the immediate postwar years as more and more easterners tried to move west. By 1952 the 870 miles of the German–German *Grenze* were no longer porous. In 1961 the last loophole, the boundary between East and West Berlin, was plugged. While the East German regime explained to its people that the Wall was necessary to keep out western militarists and fascist adventurers, we, in the West, were in no doubt the Wall was to keep the easterners in.

The thirty-some years of its existence saw several hundred people killed trying to cross fence and wall—hit by bullets, blown up by mines, or struck by the shrapnel released by automatic firing devices. More clever or lucky escapees got across hiding in secret compartments of trucks and trains, crawling through tunnels, swimming rivers, flying hang gliders or hot-air balloons, or riding in diplomats' cars. Those best situated to get away were German Democratic Republic (GDR) border guards, who could spot a momentary weakness in the system and take advantage of it. Toward the end, under pressure from Polish Solidarity and Russian glasnost as well as western opinion and Federal German Ostpolitik, some of the more murderous border armaments were taken away, but the fences and the walls lasted until the end of 1989, our *annus mirabilis*. Finally the border, clearly a Maginot Line by then, was outflanked by East Germans taking advantage of expanding freedom in Hungary and Czechoslovakia: they went "on vacation" to those once-fraternal member countries of the Cominform and Warsaw Pact, and they did not come back.

Brian Rose's photographs alert us to one of the strangest aspects of the Iron Curtain, and consequently to why we got so used to it: how unexceptional it appeared. Look at his shot of the Stubenrauchstrasse in Berlin: a quiet residential neighborhood under snow, with a woman about to climb into her car parked in an otherwise empty, snowy street (p. 81). Nothing immediately proclaims East and West. Our eye is caught first by the soft snow, at least nine inches of it, sitting on the top of the Wall like cake frosting. It is only when one takes in the Wall itself and the high, tight-mesh fence behind, and possibly notices that the car is a Russian Lada, and that the photograph is taken from a place beyond which we and the photographer cannot physically go without the chance of being shot or arrested, that it becomes clear that this is a divided world, or a fragment of it.

In an age of space rocketry, the division between the Germanies seemed old-fashioned. Of course it had ancient roots. It followed the historic boundaries of provinces such as Mecklenburg, Hanover, Saxony, and Thuringia. It was close to the line where Romans had attempted to delimit the edge of their empire with the barbarians, where Christian missionaries had once faced pagans, and Catholics and Lutherans had divided the territorial spoils. Farther south it grew ragged, almost mellowed, in Austro-Hungarian disinterest and Istrian warmth. But in our time it remained for almost four decades the border between "us" and "them," an emblem of institutionalized antipathy, a piece of cold war furniture that kept apart two sides that saw themselves as threatened by each other. Indeed, it helped preserve a situation the authorities on both sides seemed happy to live with. The fence marked the place where a balance had been found. Getting rid of it would surely disturb that delicate balance.

The border therefore was an apparatus in which various organizations had much invested. To the west, U.S. and British forces practised defensive maneuvers behind it, and West German frontier police and customs officers constantly patrolled it. To the east, GDR working parties toiled to maintain the watchtowers and death strips. Western officers saw the fence system as a wonderful "motivator"—their troops, shown this evidence of a malignant power to the east, knew why they were there.

The fence put a limit to (and made us more aware of) our western good fortune. At *Übergangs*, the crossing points, east-bound visitors waited nervously for dictatorial searches, lengthy passport examinations, and—possibly—permission to be let in. On the west, the border also became a minor tourist attraction, where gawping groups could be paraded through divided villages and led to platforms looking over into grubby East Berlin streets; schoolchildren were brought for close-at-hand educational visits. The Coke umbrellas on café terraces just west of the fence, at some *Grenzblick* (border view), flourished like banners of western

consumerism in what seemed to be the obdurately closed face of GDR puritanism.

Rose's photographs also testify marvelously to how nature persisted alongside this unnatural imposition. A pair of swans cruises peacefully on a winter stream that would be dangerous for a westerner to cross. An abundant field of West German grain grows close to the fence. Snow falls neutrally on both sides of the border, and small Baltic waves roll in similarly on beaches east and west. The great swathes of no-man's-land that the fence ran through were good for wildflowers and wildlife, for ducks, hares, pheasants, and deer. Mushroom hunters happily prowled the edges of old woods. In the little dead-end roads, lovers parked for uninterrupted trysts. Yet the border's peace was not perfect. Sometimes the watchtowers thrusting up from the ripe fields made me think of the gibbets that can be seen in some of Brueghel's landscapes, almost as natural as trees but with bodies swinging from them. The border severed families and friends, and it severed some people, fleeing the East, from life itself.

Well, it is lost—*verloren*—now, and *verschieden*—passed away. It seems a "Titanic conceit," to adopt the words of Friedrich Georg Jünger's poem *Ultima Ratio* about the end of the Nazi empire, that also suggests "everything it forged grows rusty." Robert Frost rightly observed, "Something there is that doesn't love a wall / That wants it down." Yet even before the last lumps of graffiti-covered concrete had been sold off as souvenirs and the last piece of steel-mesh fencing had been dismantled, there were those who had begun to miss it: professional soldiers hungering for firm lines on the ground; chauvinists in West Germany looking for ways of keeping out economic migrants; and, in the former GDR, those who had got a job out of it, whether as party apparatchiks or border guards. Getting rid of the division has been expensive, whether in removing wall rubble, in reopening shut lanes and reconnecting parted villages, or in plucking out the West German signs that reminded its citizens that "*Deutschland ist Unteilbar*"—Germany is indivisible. It has been particularly costly in the effort to "harmonize" two different economies, to improve the fortunes of one without overly penalizing the other. But slowly the cost of getting rid of the division has been mastered; both the envy of the easterners at western wealth and the envy of westerners at eastern doggedness in their difficult circumstances have been subsumed in a state that—if not completely *unteilbar*—is unaggressively confident now. Berlin is the capital of a single, democratic Germany again, and exhilarating with it. Rose shows us the construction equipment around the Reichstag building that now forms the country's rebuilt parliament: a splendid rebuke to the ruins of the Gestapo headquarters and the relics of Checkpoint Charlie not far away.

The Praktika cameras of the GDR *Aufklärer* (scout) patrols no longer snap malevolently along the intra-German border. Today, we are more worried about other borders, particularly the grotesque, hopeless barrier that Israel is erecting between itself and the people of Palestine. Brian Rose's memorable camerawork shows us that unloved walls ultimately come down, and what people want eventually wins out over the thick-headedness of even the most dogmatic and doctrinaire regimes.

THE LOST BORDER
BRIAN ROSE

photo: Anamarie Michnevich

I began traveling along the Iron Curtain in 1985, documenting the fences and walls of the border that divided Central Europe splitting Germany in two and tracing the western edges of Czechoslovakia, Hungary, and Yugoslavia. It felt permanent at that time, the division of the world between Soviet and American spheres of influence, though even a casual reading of the long history of this region would have suggested otherwise. As an American born in 1954 I had grown up with the cold war and its zero-sum logic—it defined my worldview, neatly symmetrical, them and us, with a nuclear trip wire in between. As a boy I had learned to duck and cover beneath my desk at school; I had watched John F. Kennedy on TV as he stood before a cheering throng in Berlin and uttered the famous line, "*Ich bin ein Berliner*"; and for years, I had kept a tattered copy of the *National Geographic* with pictures of the Berlin Wall on my bookshelf. These childhood memories and images stayed with me, and eventually, as a photographer, I set out to discover the landscape of the Iron Curtain.

In the summer of 1985 I made my first trip to Germany, flying from New York to Frankfurt with my 4x5 view camera. I rented a VW hatchback and began my journey along the great political fault line of the last half of the twentieth century. My goal to document the Iron Curtain was perhaps overly ambitious and motivated by youthful hubris, but once on the ground with my camera, I learned to focus on the immediate facts in front of me: the menacing but surprisingly banal existence of the border apparatus and its dual function as physical barrier and symbol of the cold war. I had traveled widely across the United States, a borderless world where landmarks were usually recent and transient, where people spoke the same language, and where motels and cheap food were available everywhere. In Europe I had to trade in the familiarity of roaming wide-open spaces for the reality of constantly bumping up against barriers defined by heritage, language, ideology, and nation-states. If the classic American road movie is Dennis Hopper's *Easy Rider*—two motorcyclists seeking freedom on the western landscape—the

quintessential European film of this genre is *Kings of the Road* by Wim Wenders, in which the two main characters drift along the East/West border unable to escape the physical or mental confines of history.

Although my intention was to travel the border from the Baltic Sea to the Adriatic, I decided first to visit Berlin, where the infamous Wall divided the city. Berlin's location was often mistakenly assumed to lie directly on the intra-German border where it cut across the country. It was, however, an international enclave within the German Democratic Republic (GDR), and getting there required driving or flying through tightly controlled transit corridors. My first rendezvous with the border was thus the highway, or *Autobahn*, checkpoint near Helmstedt in West Germany. Although mentally prepared for the moment, I was deeply shocked by the sight of the guard towers and automatic weapons that greeted western travelers. The scale of the operation was immense, exceeding my expectations, but I was most surprised to see that everything—the East German buildings, fortifications, vehicles, even the military uniforms—was in a state of decay. Although I had no inkling of the imminent collapse of the Soviet empire only four short years away, it was obvious to me that this was a society in decline, and that the border was provisional, not permanent.

Between 1985 and 1989, I made four trips to Europe, traveling along different stretches of the border, including numerous excursions to West Berlin. I crossed into East Berlin several times, once with my camera, but it soon became obvious that all of my photographs of the Iron Curtain would have to be taken from a western perspective. Any attempt at photographing the Wall in East Berlin would have been folly; the border guards and *Volkspolizei* (People's Police) were everywhere, and in the GDR itself, unaccompanied travel was discouraged and the border zone was off limits. Travel on the west side presented complications as well, due to the simple fact that few roadways paralleled the border. In West Germany there were hundreds of dead ends where roads once continued eastward, and I was forever zigzagging in and out along the borderline. To the south, access to the Czechoslovak, Hungarian, and Yugoslav frontiers was often difficult because of rugged terrain and dense forests. I persevered nevertheless, making use of highly detailed maps and trying every paved or reasonably maintained dirt road possible to make my way to the border.

As I drove along the frontier, I was constantly struck by the dissonance between the postcard-perfect world of Germany and Austria and the bristlingly ugly face of the border fortifications. One moment I would be squeezing my car through the picturesque walls of a medieval *Festung* (castle) or craning my neck at yet another onion-domed Baroque church; the next moment a concrete East German guard tower popped up menacingly, or a bevy of NATO helicopters streaked overhead. In the summer, the outdoor cafés were filled with prosperous burghers eating ice cream or drinking beer, seemingly oblivious to the grim dividing line that lay only a few miles away. Cozy houses with flower boxes and meticulous gardens snuggled up against the border in places, while elsewhere vast tracts of forest and field lay undeveloped on both sides of the border. Across the no-man's-land, eastern towns appeared frozen in the past; coal smoke was wisping from chimneys, and here and there the clatter of factories echoed in the otherwise still air. The border landscape was often achingly beautiful with its rolling hills and idyllic villages, and I was reminded of Claude Lanzmann's documentary film *Shoah*, in which the former sites of Nazi concentration camps were photographed in this same gloriously full-color landscape.

The GDR vigilantly maintained the border apparatus, gradually improving it and making it more efficient and effective. To the south, the fences along Czechoslovakia and Hungary were cruder, built of wooden posts and plain barbed wire instead of concrete and steel, but in all areas the border was actively patrolled. I encountered many East German guards who sometimes photographed me from their side of the border or jotted down pertinent details, presumably my car license plate number. I always worried that I would be taken aside and questioned

when entering or leaving the transit corridor to Berlin. I imagined an elaborate computer system where information about suspicious individuals was stored and could be cross-referenced but later found out that no such technology ever existed. The western border police did not pay a lot of attention to me despite my large camera and repeated presence. Border tourism was common in West Germany, with busloads of tourists stopping routinely at the many overlook platforms. In Austria I was advised by customs agents to use caution as the Czechoslovak border guards were said to be unpredictable, and in Italy the border police rather officially enforced a ban on photography in the border zone next to Yugoslavia.

The Berlin Wall and the complex of walls, fences, and watchtowers of the Iron Curtain constituted one of the unique architectural constructions in history. It lacked the monumentality of older fortifications such as the Great Wall of China, but of course its primary purpose was not to protect against enemy armies. It merely had to prevent escape and serve as a line drawn in the sand. It could be strangely beautiful, winding over hill and dale, the metal fences reflecting the sunlight reminiscent of Christo's *Running Fence*, erected in California in 1976. In Berlin, the Wall attracted Keith Haring and countless other graffiti artists, and international architects like Rem Koolhaas (OMA) and Peter Eisenman incorporated it into their designs for adjacent buildings. OMA's project, led by architect Elia Zenghelis, created an apartment building that incorporated a drive-through checkpoint on the ground floor. It was intended to replace the modest shed located in front of the building at Checkpoint Charlie, but history intervened, and the new checkpoint was never used.

I made what was supposed to be my last trip across Germany in the spring of 1989. Near Lindewerra, an East German village on the Werra River, I saw, for the first time, East German citizens wave across to western visitors. That summer, the Hungarians began rolling up their fences, and on November 9, 1989, the Berlin Wall opened, the world changed, and my project was extended. I returned to Berlin a few days before Christmas to photograph the crowds of people who had come to witness history, to chip away at the Wall, and to celebrate the New Year of 1990.

The dismantling of the Berlin Wall—some might say its wanton destruction—happened quickly, and within a couple of years only a few stretches remained. In the months before Germany was reunited in October 1990, the East Germans sold off the best pieces of graffiti-covered Wall, and the rest of the concrete and steel was crushed or recycled. Voices were raised in support of preserving significant parts of the Wall, or for marking its circuitous path through the city. But in the end the rush to rebuild the city, and the German nation, took precedence. Potsdamer Platz, which had become one of the most desolate parts of the divided city, once again stood at the crossroads of Europe and became the world's largest construction site. A new kind of tourism was born as millions of people climbed the stairs of the bright red Infobox (a temporary building set up to inform visitors of the developments in the city) to see the architectural plans and models and catch a panoramic view of the surrounding forest of cranes and rising steel. To the north, on the river Spree, new construction progressed on buildings for the relocated German government, and a glass-and-steel dome designed by Norman Foster topped the Reichstag (the seat of the German parliament), its transparency symbolizing the democratic principles of the new Germany as well as providing stirring views of the reunited city.

I visited Berlin several times during the 1990s, and then again in 2004, to photograph the reconstruction of the city, and I searched, along with other tourists, for evidence of the Wall. Ironically, one of Berlin's most sought-after tourist attractions became the wall that no longer existed physically—except in a few places—but continued to inhabit the public's imagination. Despite all the optimism about the future, German reintegration proved to be more difficult than anticipated, and many felt that something had been lost in the rapid leap forward. The newly unified capital, a showcase of glittering architecture and cultural vibrancy, faced tough economic times.

Away from Berlin, I also revisited the former intra-German borderline and found a number of guard towers still standing, maintained as memorials by local communities. At Hötensleben, a town that once stood directly on the frontier, a section of the border apparatus including a large swath of no-man's-land was preserved as a monument. The former death strip, a landscape now green and blooming with flowers, ran undisturbed, dissolving into the distance.

By the turn of the new century, the East/West border and its neatly drawn map of the world—a grand historical conceit built on twin pillars of nuclear parity—had truly vanished, and a new, dangerously muddy world had emerged. On September 11, 2001, terrorists destroyed the World Trade Center in New York, and in that event, it was clear, all vestiges of the old order were lost forever.

New York, February 2004

CURTAIN

Since the Iron Curtain was as much a political construct as a real barrier, its geography was and is often unclear to people. The Berlin Wall was only a small part of the system of fortifications that extended nearly all the way across Central Europe. The first fences were erected on the intra-German frontier in 1952, and the border elements were gradually reinforced over the years to include concrete walls, mines, automatic firing devices, and hundreds of guard towers. The division of Germany followed existing state boundaries, though here and there compromises were made to avoid splitting villages or to allow for the sharing of waterways.

To the south, along the Czechoslovak and Hungarian borders, the fences were less sophisticated but nevertheless well-guarded, and attempting escape was potentially lethal. Yugoslavia, whose Communist government remained outside the Soviet Bloc, maintained an unfenced but heavily patrolled border with its western neighbors.

Near Philippsthal the border briefly followed the Werra
River, a picturesque waterway winding past castles
and villages of half-timbered houses. The fences then
crossed the river by way of a centuries-old stone bridge
that once linked Philippsthal with Vacha, which lay to
its east in the GDR. I set up my camera near a field on
the western side, where some farmers were making hay
in the late-afternoon sun. A group of children were
playing in a street nearby, while East German guards
were watching the area from their towers.

The intra-German border consisted for the most part of double fences made of steel mesh with sharp edges. Only in the vicinity of cities and larger towns did these give way to the same concrete wall that cut through Berlin, presumably to provide more security. The steel mesh created an odd optical effect: head-on, the fences were transparent, but viewed from the side, they appeared nearly opaque. The fences and walls were always set back from the actual borderline, which was marked by posts and signs. Sometimes the border was most obviously demarcated by the fact that the grass was mowed on one side but not on the other.

35

Along the border, I frequently encountered various military patrols—the British in the north and Americans in the south—but most often I came upon the *Bundesgrenzschutz*, the West German border guards. They appeared to be primarily involved in a staring match with their East German counterparts and largely ignored my presence.

At a border overlook near the village of Müssingen, I saw two East German guards loitering at the base of a watchtower. Suddenly, they made a beeline for a gate in the fence, entered the no-man's-land, and came to a halt just a few feet across the border from me. One of them began taking pictures, while the other one turned his back as I set up my camera and photographed them.

There were three kinds of guard towers that punctuated
the border at regular intervals. The most common one
had a top-heavy form with its head sitting on a cylin-
drical base. The other towers were rectangular and
differed only in size, the larger ones serving as command
posts. Whenever I approached the border with my camera,
the East German border guards trained their binoculars
on me.

Following the border south, I drove through Bavaria, where southern Germany met Czechoslovakia. The area is mountainous and heavily forested, and I found the border to be accessible at relatively few spots. The fences were typically about a mile back from the border itself, which was marked only by a series of blue and white posts at twenty-foot intervals. Occasionally, signs warned visitors that anyone crossing the border ran the risk of arrest by the Czechoslovak authorities. Similar signs in English directed U.S. forces not to proceed without further orders.

One day while traveling this stretch of the border, I read in the paper that an East German man doing maintenance work on the border escaped near Hanover. On the same day in Berlin, twenty-nine imprisoned spies were exchanged between the U.S. and Russia over the Glienicke Bridge.

Just a few miles from the Austrian city of Gmünd, a
stretch of road paralleled the border between Czechoslovakia and Austria. The Czechoslovak fences, usually
kept far back from the borderline, here squeezed
through the city of Gmünd and its sister city, Ceské
Velenice. The fences here and elsewhere on the Czechoslovak border were relatively crude, made of wooden
posts and barbed wire, and the guard towers were often
rickety-looking wooden structures. The border was
clearly guarded by soldiers on foot, however. I saw a
number of them dressed in winter white, carrying rifles.

Near the Austrian town of Eisenberg, the Hungarian fences continued through the vineyards of the region. Further along, a small steel platform stood empty in a snowy field. In the summer of 1985, I had come across a Hungarian guard with rifle at the ready standing on this same platform watching over farm workers. It was my first trip along the border, and I could not summon the nerve to set up my camera.

To the south, the terrain once again became mountainous. I reached Dreiländereck, the point where the borders of Austria, Hungary, and Yugoslavia came together, after walking several miles through the forest.

The border between Yugoslavia and the adjacent
countries of Austria and Italy was defined by a range
of towering mountain peaks, some nearly ten thousand
feet high. I followed a beautiful winding road that
led up through the mountains to the ridge forming the
border. The best shot I found was from further down,
however, with several unusual trees breaking the
horizon in front of the peaks.

According to a local newspaper, a person fleeing
Czechoslovakia was found dead on the Yugoslav border
within Austrian territory just a few days before I took
my picture. The fugitive was apparently already in
Austria when he was shot.

WALL

After the borderline between East and West Germany
was sealed in 1952, Berlin remained an open city
governed by the World War II allies Britain, France, the
United States, and the Soviet Union. The city was a
convenient escape route for East Germans who could
easily cross into one of its western sectors until
August 13, 1961, when the GDR unexpectedly erected
the Berlin Wall. West Berlin—the British, French, and
American sectors—became an island outpost of freedom
and capitalism while the Soviet sector became East
Berlin, the communist capital of the GDR. The early
days of the city's partition were marked by dramatic
escapes, shootings, and tense standoffs between
American and Soviet tanks, as families and friends
suddenly found themselves on different sides of the
hastily constructed Wall.

By the time of my first visit to Berlin in 1985, the
Wall had become a routine fact of life in the city. Berlin
at that time was not in any sense attractive, but it had
great visual presence. The remaining prewar buildings,
often battered and scarred, and the blocks of new
apartments and office buildings created a palimpsest
of history. The great train terminals that once stood on
the periphery of Berlin Mitte were mostly destroyed,
but the subways still ran on the old tracks through
the ruined or vacant sites of the abandoned stations.
Riding on the old cars of the elevated *S-bahn*, one
could almost imagine Berlin before the war.

At the Brandenburg Gate, I took a series of photographs
of tourists posing before this historic symbol of Berlin.
It could have been a tourist sight in any city but for
the Wall blocking the way and partially obscuring the
view. Richard von Weizsäcker, mayor of West Berlin
(1981–1984) and later federal president, used to say,
"The German question remains open as long as the
Brandenburg Gate remains closed."

Alongside the Wall ran a path that was used by
many West Berliners to get from place to place on foot
or by bicycle. The Wall, while standing a few feet
within East German territory, was easily accessible,
and graffiti covered it everywhere, most abundantly
in Kreuzberg, a scruffy neighborhood of artists and
immigrants.

Near a cul-de-sac formed by a sharp turn in the Wall,
I climbed a large viewing tower. Standing among a crowd
of tourists I could observe the street life of East Berlin,
the passersby looking straight ahead or furtively
glancing our way, and the streetcars negotiating a turn-
around dictated by the Wall, which interrupted the
former through-traffic of Bernauer Strasse. Nearby, a
group of white crosses commemorating people killed
during an attempt to flee from East Berlin stood
beneath a tree.

I decided to take a break from walking the Wall one day and crossed over to East Berlin with a friend. Lichtenberg, the area we visited, was a gritty and depressing place. One house we saw was partially burnt out and partially used, but no one seemed to be around. Looking for an early modernist building listed in my guidebook, we suddenly found ourselves standing next to a huge compound of buildings equipped with video cameras. I was unnerved by the situation, especially when guards in the distance started pointing at us, so we quickly retreated down the stairs of a nearby subway station and stepped onto an arriving train. We later found out that the compound was the headquarters of the GDR secret police—the *Stasi*, or *Staatssicherheits-dienst*—essentially the CIA, FBI, and secret service rolled into one. This was certainly not a place to be walking around, particularly carrying a camera.

OPENING

In a brief series of stunning events beginning in the summer of 1989, Hungary opened its borders, and demonstrators took to the streets in East Germany demanding freedom and political reform. On November 9, the leadership of the GDR announced a new travel law allowing free movement across the border, effective immediately. Thousands of East Berliners gathered at the border checkpoints as confused guards opened the gates to West Berlin.

I arrived in Berlin in mid-December to the ringing sound of hammers and chisels. The Wall already was full of holes. Some of the so-called "wall chippers" (*Mauerspechte*) were clearly entrepreneurs filling plastic shopping bags with pieces while others seemed intent on simply hacking away at the Wall bit by bit. The crowd was a mélange of easterners and westerners—one could hear languages from all over. On Christmas Day at the Brandenburg Gate, I photographed a candle-light memorial for those killed a few days earlier in the uprising against Nicolae Ceacescu in Romania.

Berlin had changed irrevocably. The sidewalks were more crowded and the traffic heavier, as East German Trabis (short for Trabants) mixed in with the BMWs and Audis. Among the crowds, East Germans were easy to spot in their stone-washed jeans, often carrying shopping bags from western discount stores. East German border guards casually watched over the largest holes in the Wall while chatting with tourists and posing for pictures. Dozens of people were selling pieces of the Wall, and one East German man with a large display of chips on the hood of his car proudly told me that he was now a real capitalist.

Checkpoint Charlie was overflowing with auto and foot traffic. Despite the newly opened border, many tourists still stood gawking from the adjacent overlook platform. Just below, on Zimmerstrasse, the people continued to hack away at the Wall with their picks. I joined a throng of people crossing into East Berlin. Berlin Mitte was spectacularly alive—unlike anything I had seen before. The streets were teeming with people, and all the cafés and restaurants were full. In the past one's footsteps would echo in the silence of these very same streets. With the opening of the Wall, westerners had poured in just as easterners had poured out. Berlin was clearly one city again, although the border checkpoints still existed.

RUINS

I returned to Berlin in November 1990, a year after the Wall had opened and a month after the reunification of Germany. At Potsdamer Platz I came upon an odd, obviously unofficial exhibition that included fake anti-tank barriers and a stretch of the inner Wall—always kept meticulously clean by the East Germans—now marked with graffiti. Across from this weird display, a large circus tent with a blinking neon sign stood just in front of the location of the unmarked Hitler bunker. I walked to the Brandenburg Gate, which was under renovation, and down Under den Linden to the Friedrichstrasse train station, once the location of the main checkpoint into and out of East Berlin. The large glass building, known as the Palace of Tears, was now abandoned. This was where I and other travelers had been taken aside and scrutinized by blank-faced *Vopos (Volkspolizisten)* before being allowed in or out of the GDR.

Behind the Axel Springer publishing building, on some structures across the no-man's-land were various advertising billboards. A cigarette ad spelled out "Come Together," while the poster to its right was an advertisement for the PDS, the successor to the SED, the old Communist party of East Germany. It showed a young woman sticking her tongue out in joyful exuberance, and the slogan announced "Left is Alive." Nearby, graffiti on a wall read "*Keine Stasi Amnesty*" ("no amnesty for the *Stasi*," the former secret police).

It was a strange time in Berlin; a divided city was struggling to find its equilibrium. I continued to photograph along the former borderline but traveled freely about the city. Once I got into a taxi in East Berlin and asked to be taken to the Ku'damm (Kurfürstendamm), the main shopping boulevard of West Berlin. The driver, obviously an East Berliner, needed directions from me, a foreigner.

Russian soldiers were still stationed outside the city, reportedly short of food and basic supplies. One morning I read in the paper that a Russian soldier stationed in Potsdam had commandeered a tank and driven it into West Berlin down the Ku'damm. He damaged several cars in the process and was pursued by numerous police and Russian military vehicles. He was finally stopped when one of his pursuers jumped onto the tank and threw a coat over the driver's opening, obscuring his vision. Apparently, an argument between the soldier and his girlfriend had precipitated the escapade.

By the end of 1990, only a few stretches of the Wall still remained. Here and there guard towers lay toppled over, and L-shaped slabs of uprooted concrete waited to be hauled away. The Wall was vanishing almost before my eyes. An old man walking his dog watched me set up my camera in the empty no-man's-land and wondered aloud why I was taking photographs when the Wall was no longer there.

RECONSTRUCTION

In 1991 the decision was made to relocate the German
capital from its provisional home in Bonn back to
Berlin. When I visited the city in 1996, Berlin was one
big construction site. I returned to Potsdamer Platz,
where a temporary building called the Infobox informed
visitors of the developments here and elsewhere in
the city. From an observation deck I photographed a
forest of cranes rising from pits in the ground. A few
structures had begun to take form, but most would take
several years to complete. Much of the tourism in Berlin
at that time was in fact "construction-site tourism,"
a unique phenomenon where masses of people came to
the city to witness one of the largest rebuilding
campaigns in history. Two stretches of the Wall still
remained in the center of the city: one right below the
Infobox, the other between the former Luftwaffe building and the Gestapo/SS site.

At Checkpoint Charlie another burst of construction
was taking place in the open space formerly containing
customs sheds and containers. The Haus am Checkpoint Charlie, a museum dedicated to the history of the
Berlin Wall, remained as a major tourist destination.
A Philip Johnson building of dubious distinction was
under construction nearby in a complex called the
American Business Center. A golden replica of the
Statue of Liberty had been erected atop the remaining
guard tower at the checkpoint.

When I visited Berlin in 2004, the Holocaust Memorial, designed by architect Peter Eisenman, was finally under construction in the former no-man's-land between the Brandenburg Gate and Potsdamer Platz after years of discussion and controversy. Further north, along Bernauer Strasse, I photographed the Berlin Wall Memorial, a block-long stretch of wall and no-man's-land imprisoned at each end by tall steel walls, polished on one side, rusted on the other.

The development at Potsdamer Platz, which incorporates a few Wall artifacts along the former borderline, was largely completed, but at Checkpoint Charlie vacant lots remained on each side of Friedrichstrasse, evidence of the unsteady economy of the city.

REQUIEM

Adjacent to Hötensleben, a former East German town just south of Helmstedt, is a large border memorial. When I visited the site in 1996, I was shocked to see a fairway of grass where the scraped earth of the death strip used to be. The walls and fences have been preserved here, and the guard tower still stands on the crest of a hill. But even in the bright, sharp light of a fall day, the menacing face of the former border had softened through a veil of green.

Published by
Princeton Architectural Press
37 East Seventh Street
New York, New York 10003

For a free catalog of books, call 1.800.722.6657.
Visit our web site at www.papress.com.

Foreword © Anthony Bailey. Parts of this text first appeared in
Military History Quarterly.

Editing: Nicola Bednarek
Design: Joseph Plateau, Amsterdam

Special thanks to: Nettie Aljian, Janet Behning, Megan Carey,
Penny (Yuen Pik) Chu, Russell Fernandez, Jan Haux,
Clare Jacobson, John King, Mark Lamster, Nancy Eklund Later,
Linda Lee, Katharine Myers, Jane Sheinman, Scott Tennent,
Jennifer Thompson, Joseph Weston, and Deb Wood of Princeton
Architectural Press —Kevin C. Lippert, publisher

Frontispiece: Ratzeburg, East / West Germany, 1985

Library of Congress Cataloging-in-Publication Data

Rose, Brian, 1954–
 The lost border : the landscape of the Iron Curtain / Brian Rose;
foreword by Anthony Bailey.—1st ed.
    p. cm.
  ISBN 1-56898-493-6 (alk. paper)
1. Architecture—Communist countries—Pictorial works.
2. Berlin Wall, Berlin, Germany, 1961–1989—Pictorial works.
3. Architecture—Former communist countries—Pictorial works.
4. Communist countries—Boundaries—Pictorial works.
5. Former communist countries—Boundaries—Pictorial works.
6. Germany (East)—Boundaries—Germany (West)—Pictorial
works. 7. Germany (West)—Boundaries—Germany (East)—
Pictorial works. I. Title.

 D847.R67 2004
 943'.10879'0222—dc22
                                                    2004005802